GW01043848

香港的蛻變
Hong Kong The Changing Scene

歷史繪畫
A Record in Art

香港的蛻變
歷史繪畫

香港市政局主辦
Presented by the
Urban Council, Hong Kong

Hong Kong
The Changing Scene

A Record in Art

香港藝術館
Hong Kong Museum of Art
8·2·80 — 9·3·80

市政局
Urban Council

ISBN 962-215-023-3
Published by the Urban Council, 1980
Produced by the Hong Kong Museum of Art

UC 10450
HK$32.00

EXHIBITION MANAGEMENT

Curator:	Laurence C.S. Tam
Assistant Curator I:	Chui Yin-har, Eliza
Assistant Curators II	
Historical Pictures:	Joseph S.P. Ting
Publication Design:	Irene Kho
Exhibition Graphics:	Winnie Kwan
Photography:	Vincent Chan

Introduction

Before the introduction of the camera in the 1860s to the Far East, the only means available for capturing the sights and scenes of its people and places was by means of drawing and painting — as indeed was the case in the rest of the world too. Some of these drawings and paintings, often made with no thought of posterity, fortunately survive, and through them we can see what Hong Kong looked like at various times in the past, and thus also discover something of how, visually, it changed.

In the early 19th century, European vessels going to China often came to Hong Kong not for commercial reasons but simply to call at a pretty little waterfall west of Aberdeen to obtain water before proceeding up the Pearl River to Whampoa and Canton. Such a scenic spot has been so much altered through construction work around it, that the original appearance of the falls might not now be known, had it not been for a small watercolour, attributed to W. Havell,[1] circa 1816, which survived in the former Sayer collection, and is now in the Hong Kong Museum of Art. This miniature watercolour, possibly the earliest pictorial record of Hong Kong still extant, depicts a small boat going for the water shown pouring over the cliffs at Waterfall Bay near Aberdeen. This picture was later transformed into a print by T. Fielding. Hong Kong as seen in this picture was an island of barren rocks, deep ravines and mountain torrents. (Plate No. 1) According to Clarke Abel, the surgeon of Lord Amherst's Embassy, the inhabitants in Hong Kong at that time were a few fishermen.[2]

For more information on Hong Kong in the early 19th century we owe much to the records in both written and pictorial form by a young French artist Auguste Borget who arrived at Hong Kong on board the ship *Psyche* on 23rd August 1838. He made some drawings and watercolours depicting local rural life and village scenes during his short sojourn, thus giving us a vivid picture of how Hong Kong looked before 1841.[3] (Plates No. 2-6)

The development of Hong Kong from a barren and rocky island to a promising seaport in the 19th century seemed a miracle to some visitors. To put it in James Legge's words, 'One must travel far to find another spot where human energy and skill have triumphed to such an extent over difficulties of natural position.'[4] In fact, the rapid progress of Hong Kong was and has been the result of the remarkable diligence and endurance of her inhabitants in overcoming difficulties and hardships, whether they be derived from human or natural factors.

In June 1841, the first official sale of land by auction took place[5] and this was followed by large-scale building of godowns and houses. Places first opened up for commercial and residential purposes included East Point, Happy Valley, Spring Gardens, Canton Bazaar (near the present Naval Yard in Queensway), West Point, the slope below Wyndham Street, Pottinger Street, Queen's Road and Sai Ying Pun.

This newly-developed settlement continued to progress despite setbacks brought by epidemics of fever, and financial problems. Captain Arthur Cunynghame, who arrived at Hong Kong in August 1841 and returned in June 1842, remarked, 'Perhaps no place in the history of ages can boast of such a rapid rise as the town of Hong Kong.'[6] In 1846, in a passage written about Hong Kong in his writings on China, the first Bishop of Victoria, Rev. George Smith, has the following description: 'The rugged precipitous shore, which forms the southern edge of the harbour, presents the imposing aspect of a European town suddenly grown into existence, with regular streets of substantial buildings, rising one above another. . . . Many of the buildings in the new town are of significant structure, raised at an enormous expense, by cutting away the sides of the projecting headlands. The more western parts of the town are occupied by Chinese streets and bazaars, which have been raised with wonderful rapidity, and contain a busy and enterprising portion of the community. The native population of the island having been already nearly trebled. . . .'[7]

The rapid development as described by these writers is vividly shown in many of the paintings and prints done by different artists of that period. (Plates 10, 11, 13, 15 and 16) The most famous of these are perhaps the chromolithographs drawn by Murdoch Bruce, an Inspector of Buildings in the

1840s. This set of twelve prints shows the views of different parts of the newly established settlement including the City of Victoria, Spring Gardens, East Point, Sai Wan and Aberdeen. (Plates 17-28) These pictures are valuable visual records of Hong Kong, and they complement many written records that have survived. A comparison of Bruce's and Borget's lithographs gives some idea of how much Hong Kong changed within the span of a decade.

The period from 1841 to 1855 in Hong Kong was an era of construction. Queen's Road, built along a well-marked track facing the harbour along the northern shore all the way from West Point to East Point, was completed early in the period. This road, said to have been called 'Petticoat String Road' by the Chinese in the early days, has been a main thoroughfare ever since. (Plate 26) A number of important landmarks were also built within this period, namely, Murray House and Headquarter House in 1845, the old Hong Kong Club in 1846, the Government Offices in 1847, St. John's Cathedral in 1849, Bishop's House in 1851, and Government House in 1855. We are grateful to an anonymous artist who, about 1854, portrayed in an oil painting the view of Victoria City and the harbour in great detail with the shape and location of these landamarks accurately and faithfully executed. (Plate 33) The picture conveys the message that Hong Kong was a busy seaport and had grown into a thriving city by around 1854.

Overseas trade depends much on sea transport; so the growth of Hong Kong's trade has been very closely related to the development of shipping lines. Hong Kong enjoyed a boom in the shipping business in the period between 1860 and the 1870s when the Ben Line, Messageries Maritimes, Pacific Mail, and Blue Funnel lines all began regular services to the Far East.[8] In the oil paintings and watercolours showing the harbour of this period, it is often seen to be congested with a great variety of ships. (Plates 41, 47 and 48)

In connection with shipping, ship-building and godowns also underwent rapid development at the same time. In 1863, a large strong timber pier in Hong Kong was erected at Spring Gardens for the godowns of McGregor & Co.. It is interesting to note that all former piers had been probably built of bamboo. The Aberdeen Docks were kept fully at work from 1860 to 1863. In 1866 the Hong Kong and Whampoa Dock Company was established. An indication of economic progress was also reflected by the opening of the Hong Kong and Shanghai Banking Corporation in 1864, and the Mint of Hong Kong in 1866.[9] (Plate 42)

The 1870s saw the eastward movement of Chinese merchants into the Central District. Before then, most Chinese lived in a half square mile area west of Wen Wu Temple, between Tai Ping Shan Street and Possession Street, whereas the Europeans were concentrated in the area east of Aberdeen Street. However, in the latter part of the 1870s, Chinese merchants began to penetrate into the central district of the town, hitherto regarded by custom as the exclusive preserve of the Europeans. A comparison of Murdoch Bruce's *View of Lyndhurst Terrace, Wellington Street and Cochrane Street Looking West from the Roman Catholic Chapel* (Plate 17) with C. Andrasi's *View of Wellington Street,* (Plate 51) which were drawn in 1846 and in the 1870s respectively, clearly reveals the above fact.

During the 1870s, buildings on the Peak also multiplied and it began to be widely popular as a summer resort. However, it was the opening of the Peak Tram in 1888 which gave an active stimulus to the development of the upper levels. This change can also be traced in the paintings exhibited.

One of the most significant events in the 1890s was the construction of the New Praya, suggested and planned by C.P. Chater in 1887. It was begun in 1890 and completed in 1904, and, the Old Praya was then renamed Des Voeux Road.[10] An oil painting by an anonymous artist in about 1902 shows that the reclamation scheme for the New Praya was underway. (Plate 55)

Due to the perishable nature of paper and canvas, many of the depictions of old Hong Kong in oils, watercolours and drawings by professionals and amateurs alike have vanished. Fortunately, many of the original images of old Hong Kong were also reproduced in prints in the form of lithographs, etchings, mezzotints and woodblocks. For instance, when James Orange was compiling his catalogue, *The Chater Collection,* in 1924, although he could not locate Havell's watercolour of the waterfall, he was able to reproduce an aquatint of it by T. Fielding. It is not strange, therefore, that we find that the majority of our exhibits are prints.

The fifty-eight items on display include thirty-four prints, seven oils, sixteen watercolours and one drawing, all selected from the collection of historical pictures in the Hong Kong Museum of Art. This collection has been built up mainly from the Hotung Collection, the Chater Collection, and the Law and Sayer Collections, plus new additions through acquisitions in recent years. While some are fine works by known artists like Auguste Borget, Murdoch Bruce and Marciano Baptista (a pupil of George Chinnery), many of them are anonymous or by amateurs whose history cannot be traced. The earliest picture in this exhibition is dated 1816 and the latest 1926, and within these eleven decades, much more had taken place than is revealed by them, for the collection as it stands is far from being complete in representing the whole changing scene of Hong Kong during the period in question.

This selection of pictures shows some of the dramatic changes in the appearance of Hong Kong and something of the artistic styles of the 19th and early 20th centuries. The catalogue is an initial attempt to illuminate some significant features and points of special interest in the exhibits. We hope that this will serve as a basis for future research on the subject.

We are grateful to many who have contributed their assistance in the preparation of this exhibition, especially for the expert advice given by our Honorary Museum Advisers, Mr. Geoffrey Bonsall, and Mr. Nigel Cameron, and the Archivist of the Hong Kong Public Records Office, Mr. Ian Diamond. Without their support, this catalogue would never have been produced.

Laurence C.S. Tam
Curator
Hong Kong Museum of Art
December, 1979

Notes

1 James Orange in *The Chater Collection* mentions T. Fielding as the artist of the print of the picture in question without mentioning the name of the artist responsible for the original picture. According to the records of the Sayer collection, the watercolour is attributed to W. Havell.

2 James Orange, *The Chater Collection*, 1924, p. 324.

3 Auguste Borget, *Sketches of China and the Chinese*, pp. 2 and 3, plates III -VI.

4 Nigel Cameron, *The Cultured Pearl*, 1978, pp. 36 and 37.

5 E.J. Eitel, *Europe in China, the History of Hong Kong, from the Beginning to the Year 1882*, 1895, pp. 172-174. The following is Eitel's description of the result of that auction: '.... But it was found impossible to survey and stake out, in time for the sale, more than 40 lots, all situated along the shore, north of Queen's Road, and having each a sea frontage of 100 feet. Six of these lots were reserved for the Crown, one remained unsold, but the remaining 33 lots, put up at an upset price of £10, were sold (June 14, 1841) at an average rate of £71, prices ranging from £20 to £265 per lot.'

6 James Orange, *The Chater Collection*, 1924, P. 334

7 Ibid, p. 337. The full title of Smith's work is *A Narrative of an Exploratory Visit to Each of the Consular Cities of China and to the Islands of Hong Kong and Chusan, in behalf of the Church Missionary Society in the Years 1844-1845-1846*. The Rev. George Smith was appointed the first Bishop of Hongkong in 1850 and died in 1871.

8 Lin Yu-lan, *Hsiang-kiang shi hua*, 1978, pp. 50-51.

9 The dates quoted in this paragraph are based on E.J. Eitel, *Europe in China, the History of Hong Kong, from the Beginning to the Year 1882*, 1895.

10 G.B. Endacott, *A History of Hong Kong*, 1978, p. 210.

序

　　攝影機是在一八六〇年代傳到遠東來的。在此之前，要記錄人們的生活狀態及地方的外貌，祇有倚靠繪畫。此種情形，在世界各地均如是。此等經歷時變而尚能保存下來的繪畫，使我們能目睹當年香港的面貌，從而探索其蛻變的過程，這倒是繪畫者當初所意料不到的。

　　十九世紀初期，訪華的船隻多寄碇於石排灣以西海面，並從附近的一條瀑布補充食水，然後才沿珠江直航黃埔或廣州。由於歷年來城市建設的發展，此瀑布附近的環境已全面改觀，幸得一幅相傳為哈維（註一）在一八一六年所繪畫，描寫海員刘小艇到瀑布旁汲水的情景的水彩畫，能把當時的景象保留下來。這可能是現存描繪香港景色最早的繪畫，原屬塞耶舊藏，現為香港藝術館藏品。該畫在早年由菲爾丁轉刻為版畫。從是圖所見，當時的香港一片荒涼，四野盡是岩石深谷，瀑流滾滾。（圖片1）據阿美士德使節團的隨團醫生艾貝爾的描述，當時香港的居民多以捕魚為生，人口寥寥可數。（註二）

　　一位年青的法國畫家波塞爾在一八三八年八月廿三日乘「西奇」號輪抵港。留港期間，他繪畫了數幅水彩及素描，分別描繪了當時的鄉村生活及漁村景色，使我們能看到本港在一八四一年前的面貌。（圖片2至6）波塞爾還以文字記錄了他在港的所見所聞。（註三）

　　在十九世紀期間，香港從一個荒僻的小島發展為繁榮的商港，到港訪客無不視為奇蹟。著名漢學家理雅各說：「要找尋另外一個像香港般能具體地反映出人類充份發揮其體能與技巧以克服自然環境的地方，委實不易。」（註四）事實上，本港能有今天的成就，乃是刻苦耐勞的本港居民長期艱苦奮鬥的成果。

　　一八四一年六月，港府首次拍賣官地。（註五）大規模的貨倉及房屋建設，遂告展開。最早被關作商業及住宅用途的區域有：東角、黃泥涌、春園、廣州市場（今金鐘道舊海軍船塢附近）、西環、雲咸街附近斜坡、砵甸乍街、皇后道及西營盤。

　　儘管當時受到流行熱病的蹂躪及財政困難，早期的香港仍穩步前進。阿瑟·坎尼威在一八四一年八月過港。翌年六月，故地重遊，對本港的飛躍發展深表驚訝。他說：「香港發展之迅速，實在史無前例！」（註六）一八四六年，香港教區第一位會督喬治·史密斯牧師在其記述中國之行的名作中有如下的描述：「海港南面陡峭的海岸，呈現一個看似歐陸的市鎮。整齊的街道，穩固的房屋，一層層的沿著山坡興建……新市鎮中的很多建築物都非常壯觀，營造工程浩大，甚至要夷平部份山坡。港島西部是華人聚居之地，街道及市場，發展迅速，繁盛喧鬧。華人比前增加幾達三倍……」。（註七）

　　上述關於香港迅速發展的評語，可從這一時期畫家的繪畫中得以證實（圖片10、11、13、15及16）。其中尤以布魯士的設色石版畫，最具代表性。布魯士在一八四〇年代曾任香港的建築物督察。通過此一套共十二幀的石版畫，布魯士生動地介紹了當時的維多利亞城、春園、東角、西灣及香港仔等地的風光。（圖片17至28）此等圖畫，既保留了本港舊貌的紀錄，更可補充早期訪港旅客所寫下有關本港的文字記載。如果把波塞爾和布魯士的石版畫作一比較，本港在開埠前後間的巨大變化，更能一目了然。

　　一八四一年至一八五五年期間，是香港早期重要的建設時代。首先，沿著港島北岸蜿蜒伸展的一條名為「裙帶路」的小徑，被擴闊為皇后大道。此路自此成為港島的交通動脈。很多著名的早期建築物都是在這個年代興建的，包括美利樓及旗杆屋（建於一八四五年）；舊香港會所（建於一八四六年）；輔政司署（建於一八四七年）；聖約翰教堂（建於一八四九年）；會督府（建於一八五一年）和督憲府（建於一八五五年）等。一幅完成於一八五四年間的油畫，描繪了當年的維多利亞港的景色。而上述的著名建築物多可見於圖中。（圖片33）該畫的內容反映出香港在一八五四年間已成為一個繁忙的港口及具規模的城市。

　　本港商業發達與航運業的蓬勃是息息相關的。一八六〇年至一八七〇年代的一段時間，本港的航運業突趨興旺。法國郵船公司、太平洋郵船公司、邊行及藍烟囱輪船公司紛紛拓展其航運至遠東。（註八）因此，在這時期的油畫及水彩畫，很多是繪寫港海內帆檣如林的景象。（圖片41、47及48）。

　　與此同時，本港的造船業及貨倉業也日趨蓬勃。一八六三年，位於春園的麥奇利哥公司的貨倉，築起一座用木材建築的新碼頭。據說在此以前的碼頭均是以竹棚架設的。石排灣造船廠在一八六〇年至六三年間的生意奇佳，大有應接不暇之勢。一八六六年，香港黃埔船塢公司成立。此外，在一八六〇年代創立的金融機構，包括香港上海滙豐銀行（一八六四年）及香港造幣廠（一八六六年）等，都足以反映當年香港商業經濟蓬勃的一斑。（註九）

在一八七〇年代，華商的活動開始向東拓展。開埠初期，華人多聚居於文武廟以西，即太平山街及水坑口一帶方圓半哩的區域，而鴨巴甸街以東則全屬洋人天下。此形勢維持到一八七〇年代。當時中國商人向東推移，收購不少洋人物業。這種現象可從布魯士在一八四六年所繪畫的「從羅馬天主堂西眺擺花街、威靈頓街及閣麟街」（圖片17）與安德烈西在一八七〇年代所繪畫的「威靈頓街一景」（圖片51）互相比較下，可窺見一二。

在一八七〇年代期間，山頂的建築逐漸增加，並有以該處為夏天避暑勝地的。一八八八年，山頂纜車啟行，加速了山頂區的開發。移居山頂的人更趨普遍。在此段時期完成的繪畫亦多反映出此一事實。

一八九〇年代，中區沿岸進行龐大的填海工程，建設了一新的海旁。該工程乃由遮打爵士在一八七七年所建議及策劃，於一八九〇年開始施工，而於一九〇四年完成。竣工後，原來的舊海旁遂改稱為德輔道。（註十）一位不知名的畫家約於一九〇二年間繪畫了一幅油畫，為我們把建築新海旁時的香港景象記錄下來。（圖片55）

紙張及帆布皆容易破爛，因此，許多描繪香港舊貌的油畫、水彩及素描畫因年代湮遠而未能保存下來。此等歷史繪畫包括了職業及業餘畫家的作品。由於版畫印製技術早已流行，舊香港的面貌遂得以藉石版畫、蝕刻畫、金屬版畫及木版畫等保存下來。當詹姆士‧奧倫治在一九二四年編寫其不朽巨著「遮打氏藏畫集」時，便因為未能找到哈維畫的「香港仔附近的瀑布」一畫的水彩原作，而不得不選用菲爾丁所轉刻的飛塵蝕刻版畫。歷史繪畫原作保存不易，故是次所展覽的，亦以版畫為多。

是次展出的五十八幀畫作，包括三十四幅版畫、七幅油畫、十六幅水彩及一幅素描，全部均由香港藝術館所藏歷史繪畫中選出。其中不少是原屬何東、遮打、塞耶及勞氏藏畫中的珍品，也包括了本館近年所增購的歷史圖畫。其中有如波塞爾、布魯士及巴普蒂斯塔（錢納利的學生）等名畫家的作品，也有一些是由佚名或業餘畫家所繪畫。可惜很多此等畫家的生平已無從稽考。展品的年代從一八一六年至一九二六年。本港在這一百一十年間的重大演變，當非數十幀圖畫所能盡載。而本館所藏亦只能代表現存散處各地的香港歷史圖畫的部份而已。

是次展出的歷史圖畫，目的是透過十九及二十世紀早期的畫作以觀賞本港蛻變過程的大概。本目錄試對展品內容作簡短的描述。這是一個初步的嘗試，希望能引起更多人士對此等畫的內容作進一步的研究。

本展覽籌備期間，承蒙各友好支持與協助，藝術館名譽顧問彭傑福先生、金馬侖先生及香港政府檔案處主任戴雅文先生不時提供寶貴意見，俾本目錄得以順利編製完成。本館全寅謹藉此向他們致以衷心的謝意。

譚志成
香港藝術館館長
一九七九年十二月

註釋

註一　在 *The Chater Collection* 一書中，James Orange 沒有交代誰是該畫的原作者，祇指出菲爾丁爲該版畫的作者。根據塞耶藏畫的紀錄，此水彩畫傳爲哈維所作。

註二　參閱 James Orange, *The Chater Collection*，一九二四年版，頁三二四。

註三　參閱 Auguste Borget, *Sketches of China and the Chinese*，頁二及三，圖三至六。

註四　參閱 Nigel Cameron, *The Cultured Pearl*，一九七八年版，頁三六及三七。

註五　參閱 E.J. Eitel, *Europe in China, the History of Hong Kong, from the Beginning to the Year 1882*，一八九五年版，頁一七二至一七四。以下爲 Eitel 對是次官地競投的記載：「……能及時完成勘探和劃分的地段，可提供該次拍賣的也只不過四十幅，全部位於皇后道以北的海旁。每一段均佔有一百英呎的海岸。其中除六幅地段留作官方之用和一幅沒有售出外，其餘的三十幅地段均以底價十英鎊開投（時在一八四一年六月十四日），結果分別以二十英鎊至二百六十五英鎊的價錢投出。平均每幅值七十一英鎊。」

註六　參閱 James Orange, *The Chater Collection*，一九二四年版，頁三三四。

註七　同上，頁三三七。史密斯會督的巨著全名爲：*A Narrative of an Exploratory Visit to Each of the Consular Cities of China and to the Islands of Hong Kong and Chusan, in behalf of the Church Missionary Society in the Year: 1844-1845-1846*。喬治‧史密斯在一八五〇年被委任爲香港教區第一任會督。他在一八七一年去世。

註八　參閱林友蘭：「香港史話」一九七八年版，頁五〇至五一。

註九　本段所有年份俱出自 E. J. Eitel, *Europe in China, the History of Hong Kong, from the Beginning to the Year 1882*，一八九五年版。

註十　參閱 G. B. Endacott, *A History of Hong Kong*，一九七八年版，頁二一〇。

List of Plates

圖版目錄

22

Plates 圖版

1 The Waterfall at Hong Kong, circa 1816
   attributed to W. Havell
   watercolour, 10.5 × 16 cm

1 香港仔附近的瀑布，約一八一六年
   傳爲哈維所作
   水彩畫　10.5×16公分

This waterfall at Shek Pai Wan near Aberdeen on the southwest coast of Hong Kong Island was well known to foreign sailors as a reliable place for replenishing their ships' stocks of water. The waterfall is still visible near to the present Wah Fu Housing Estate, but the flow of water was much reduced when the Pokfulam Reservoir was constructed.

The watercolour was reproduced as the frontispiece to Geoffrey Robley Sayer, *Hong Kong: Birth, Adolescence and Coming of Age,* 1937, and a mezzotint by T. Fielding is used for the frontispiece of Clarke Abel, *Narrative of a Journey in the Interior of China,* London, 1818. The mezzotint is also described and illustrated in James Orange, *The Chater Collection,* 1924, pp.348 and 371.

十九世紀初期來華貿易船隻多寄碇於石排灣西南海面，並在今華富邨附近一條瀑布汲水飲用。該瀑布迄今尚存，但在薄扶林水塘建成後，已因流水減弱而變爲一條山溪。

此圖也見於　Geoffrey Robley Sayer, *Hong Kong: Birth, Adolescence and Coming of Age,* 一九三七年出版的卷首插圖。另一幅菲爾丁所印製的金屬版畫則在 Clarke Abel, *Narrative of a Journey in the Interior of China,* 一八一八年倫敦出版一書中作卷首插圖。此幅金屬版畫的詳細描述，見於 James Orange, *The Chater Collection,* 一九二四年出版，頁三四八及三七一。

2　Bay and Island of Hong Kong, 1838
by Auguste Borget, 1809 - 1877, lithographed by E. Ciceri
coloured lithograph, 29 × 41 cm

2　港島及海灣，一八三八年
波塞爾畫（一八〇九至一八七七），西塞里刻印
設色石版畫　29×41公分

This is one of the 32 scenes used to illustrate the English and French editions of Borget's book, *Sketches of China and the Chinese.* Some of these have been reproduced as a separate series. Borget describes each view in detail in his book. About this one, dated August 1838, he says: '. . . The next day I landed on the north-east, close by a promontory, where there are several houses, to which are attached wheels, for the purpose of withdrawing the fishing nets, and which give the place quite a peculiar character. . .' Borget's work has also been copied in several other books, e.g. Allom and Wright's, *China in a Series of Views.*
See also Plates 3, 4 and 5 and James Orange, *The Chater Collection*, pp. 351 and 376; Nigel Cameron, *Hong Kong, the Cultured Pearl*, 1978, p.49.

此爲波塞爾的「中國及中國人素描集」所收集的三十二幅作品中的一幅，見於其書之英法版本。此等作品，皆已刻印爲石版畫。在前述書籍中，波塞爾對其所繪畫的每一幅作品，均有詳盡記述；他於一八三八年八月，對此圖有如下的描述：「翌日，我在東北岸登陸，那裏是個海角，附近有不少房屋，屋外有用來收漁網的轉輪，饒有趣味……。」波塞爾的作品，曾收錄在不少書籍中，例如 Allom 及 Wright, *China in a Series of Views* 便是。
此可與圖3、4及5比較，並可參閱James Orange, *The Chater Collection,* 頁三五一及三七六；Nigel Cameron, *Hong Kong, The Cultured Pearl,* 一九七八年出版，頁四九。

3 A Bamboo Aqueduct, Hong Kong, 1838
   by Auguste Borget, 1809-1877, lithographed by E. Ciceri
   coloured lithograph, 19 × 28.5 cm

From Borget's *Sketches of China and the Chinese*. Borget wrote: 'This part of the valley has only a narrow opening towards the seashore. In the middle of this little gorge stands a large mass of rock. On the summit they have formed a little canal, and placing at each extremity a pipe formed of bamboo, have thus constructed an aqueduct to convey the water across the valley, and so fertilised places which, without such an expedient, had been condemned to eternal sterility.'
See also James Orange, *The Chater Collection*, pp. 350 and 375. This picture has also been differently engraved as a book illustration, for example, in Allom and Wright's, *China in a Series of Views*.

3 香港的竹製導水管，一八三八年
   波塞爾畫（一八〇九至一八七七），西塞里刻印
   設色石版畫　19×28.5公分

波塞爾在「中國及中國人素描集」中，對此圖畫有如下的描述：「此部份山谷，僅有一個狹窄的出口可通向海邊，峽口有一巨石，在岡頂的兩邊，有一條引水道，由一條橫互於巨石上的竹製導水管接連，把水導引到一塊荒瘠的土地，作灌溉之用。」
可參閱 James Orange, *The Chater Collection*, 頁三五〇及三七五。是畫曾刻印作爲書籍插圖。參閱 Allom 及 Wright, *China in a Series of Views*.

4 A Village Square on the Island of Hong Kong, 1838
by Auguste Borget, 1809-1877, lithographed by E. Ciceri
coloured lithograph, 28.5 × 40.5 cm

4 港島某村莊小廣場，一八三八年
波塞爾畫（一八〇九至一八七七），西塞里刻印
設色石版畫　28.5×40.5公分

In his book, Borget describes how he drew this picture. 'I advanced to the
middle part of the street, and stationing myself opposite the temple,
under an immense tree, whose roots stretched out on every side, I
commenced sketching and was soon surrounded by gazers.'
See also James Orange, *The Chater Collection*, pp. 352 and 378.

波塞爾對此圖作如下的描述：「我走到街道的中央，站在一幢廟宇的
對面，在一棵樹根向四面伸展的大樹下，我開始寫生，但迅即爲好奇
的村民所包圍。」
可參閱　James Orange, *The Chater Collection*, 頁三五二及三七八。

5 Fishing Junks and Sampans, Kowloon, 1838
  by Auguste Borget, 1809-1877, lithographed by E. Ciceri
  coloured lithograph, 28.5 × 41.3 cm

Borget wrote in his book: 'One morning I crossed the bay and landed in a little creek, where there is a village of boats drawn ashore, a kind of habitation of which we have no idea in Europe. . . . Some of these boat-houses are sheltered under large trees, others leaning against the rocks, but the greater part rest on the ground, supported by stays. . .'.
See also James Orange, *The Chater Collection*, pp. 352 and 377.

5 九龍灣的住家艇，一八三八年
  波塞爾畫（一八〇九至一八七七），西塞里刻印
  設色石版畫　28.5×41.3公分

波塞爾寫道：「一天早上，我越過港灣，來到一條小溝旁，岸邊擺滿住家艇，此種居住方式是我們在歐洲聞所未聞的⋯⋯有些住家艇擱在大樹下，有些背靠着大石，更多是以支索支撐，架在地上。」
可參閱 James Orange, *The Chater Collection*, 頁三五二及三七七。

6 Fishing Boat and Figures, Hong Kong, 1838
  by Auguste Borget, 1809-1877
  pencil drawing, 11.5 × 18.5 cm
  signed

6 港島的漁船及漁民，一八三八年
  波塞爾（一八〇九至一八七七）
  鉛筆素描　11.5×18.5公分
  附有畫家署名

Original pencil drawings by Borget are much rarer than engravings and oils. They all show a strong influence of George Chinnery and there is proof that they met during Borget's visit to Hong Kong and Macao.

此乃波塞爾的鉛筆素描原作，故比他其他的石版畫或油畫珍貴。波塞爾曾在旅遊香港及澳門時，與錢納利相晤，波氏作品的風格顯然受到錢氏畫風的影响。

7 Early View of Hong Kong Island, 1841
by John H. Collins
watercolour, 20.5 × 27 cm

7 港島遠眺，一八四一年
柯林斯
水彩畫　20.5×27公分

Building developed quickly after the occupation of Hong Kong Island in 1841. This view shows the beginnings of the central area with some houses and possibly a military encampment, and some more buildings to the east, but very little vegetation. Eight naval vessels are clearly shown with several junks in the foreground.

在一八四一年，香港開埠數月間，各類型建築物開始湧現。是圖所見乃中區的景象，房屋不多，但可見軍隊已在岸邊駐紮。圖左方還有一些建築，但樹木不多。港內泊了八艘船隻，前方還可看到數艘漁舟。

8 Fort Victoria, Kowloon, May 1841
   by John H. Collins
   watercolour, 22.5 × 32 cm
   signed

An unusually detailed view of the fortifications to the west of Tsim Sha Tsui, showing buildings in Chinese style surrounded by a thick granite wall. The two small houses on the Point are also shown in no. 31. A view of a part of this Fort is shown in no. 9.

8 尖沙咀的九龍炮台，一八四一年五月
   柯林斯
   水彩畫　22.5×32公分
   附有畫家署名

畫中所見乃位於尖沙咀西面的九龍炮台。該炮台牆垣頗厚，乃以大麻石所砌成，炮樓爲中國式。尖沙咀尖端有兩間小屋，在圖31也可看到，圖9爲此炮台的近景。

Fort Victoria Hong Kong
May 1841 J.H.C.

9 Fort Victoria, Kowloon, circa 1841
   by M.J. Starling, engraver, from drawing of Thomas Allom, after sketch
   by Lieutenant White
   engraving, 12.7 × 19 cm

9 尖沙咀九龍炮台近景，約一八四一年
   艾龍根據懷特少校的素描所繪畫，斯特林刻印
   金屬刻版畫　12.7×19公分

A detail of part of the fortification shown in no. 8, with British soldiers on
guard, paddle-wheel steamer and sailing ships in the background, and
trading junks in the foreground.
Illustration from Allom and Wright, *China in a Series of Views*. See James
Orange, *The Chater Collection*, pp. 354 and 379.

此爲圖 8 尖沙咀砲台的近景。砲台上有英兵站崗，遠方有美式輪船及
數艘商船；前方還可看見中國帆船。
此圖乃 Allom 及 Wright, *China in a Series of Views* 一書的插圖。
可參閱 James Orange, *The Chater Collection*, 頁三五四及三七九。

10 Victoria and Hong Kong from the Northeast, 1843
by J. Prendergast, engraved by E. Duncan
aquatint, 25.5 × 36.5 cm

A view from the northeast of Kellett Island, named after Sir Henry
Kellett, showing East Point and Jardine, Matheson & Co's godowns, with
Morrison Hill behind and extensive building along the waterfront with
the Harbour Master's house and flagstaff on the hill behind. Kellett
Island, also known as Lantern Island, Tang Lung Chau in Chinese, is no
longer an island, and the whole area has been reclaimed and developed
and now includes the entrance to the cross-harbour tunnel.
A series of views by Prendergast was announced in the *Canton Press* of
1843 but only this item and no. 11 are now known. See also James
Orange, *The Chater Collection*, pp. 356 and 384.

10 港島東北岸景色，一八四三年
普倫德加斯特畫，鄧肯刻印
設色蝕刻版畫　25.5×36.5公分

此圖左方為東角渣甸洋行及貨倉，東角後方為摩利臣山，沿岸有不少
建築物，遠處可看見位於小岡上的港務官辦事處及其旗杆；海岸對開
的小島是奇力島（又名燈籠洲），乃因紀念奇力爵士而命名。奇力島
現已與港島北岸接連，並成為海底隧道出口所在。
普倫德加斯特的一些畫作曾在一八四三年的廣州報刊上刊登，但除圖
11及此圖外，餘皆散佚。可參閱 James Orange, *The Chater Collection*
頁三五六及三八四。

11 Kellett Island and Hong Kong from the Northeast, 1843
by J. Prendergast, engraved by E. Duncan
aquatint, 25.5 × 36.5 cm

This closely resembles no. 10 but the buildings on Hong Kong Island and the fort show variations.   Kellett Island became a fort and is now the location of the Royal Hong Kong Yacht Club.
See also James Orange, The *Chater Collection*, pp. 356-357 and 385; Nigel Cameron, *Hong Kong, the Cultured Pearl*, p. 15

11 從東北方眺望奇力島及香港景色，一八四三年
普倫德加斯特畫，鄧肯刻印
設色蝕刻版畫 25.5×36.5公分

此圖與圖10相似，但圖中所見港島及奇力島的建築物均略有不同。奇力島曾建有堡壘，現已成為皇家香港遊艇會的基地。
可參閱 James Orange, *The Chater Collection*, 頁三五六、三五七及三八五，與及 Nigel Cameron, *Hong Kong, the Cultured Pearl*,頁十五。

12 Wong Nei Chong, early 1840s
artist unknown
coloured lithograph, 22.8 × 33 cm

This rare view of Happy Valley looking north shows the Morrison Education Society building on Morrison Hill to the left, probably Mercer's house on the right and foreign shipping in the harbour, with stonemasons and a quarry in the foreground above the village of Wong Nei Chong.

12 黃泥涌一景，一八四〇年代早期
畫家佚名
設色石版畫　22.8×33公分

此乃自黃泥涌北眺港海景色，左方的小岡爲摩利臣山，其上建築物爲馬禮遜教育會；右方或爲默塞爾住宅，港海內有數艘洋船；圖中前方爲一採石廠，位於黃泥涌村之上。

13 East Point, Hong Kong, early 1840s
artist unknown
coloured lithograph, 16 × 23.5 cm

An unusual view of East Point and an interesting comparison with nos. 10 and 15. The shallow water of the bay is being prepared for a road and a granite seawall is shown under construction.

13 香港東角，一八四〇年代早期
畫家佚名
設色石版畫　16×23.5公分

圖中可見工人正忙於興建道路及海堤；此圖描繪東角景色，與圖10及15相似，均可參看。

14 A Chinese Temple, Hong Kong Island, early 1840s.
artist unknown
lithograph, 15.5 × 22.5 cm

14 港島一廟宇，一八四〇年代早期
畫家佚名
石版畫　15.5×22.5公分

An unusual view of the southern side of Hong Kong Island showing Chinese figures and stone lions outside a temple probably at Stanley, which was named after Lord Stanley, the Secretary of State for the Colonies at the time. Stanley (or Chek-chu) was one of the early villages on the island and had a population of fishermen and farmers.

此圖所見乃港島南岸某廟宇之景，地點可能在赤柱。廟門有石獅一對，香客甚衆。赤柱英名史丹利，以紀念十九世紀英國殖民地大臣史丹利爵士。赤柱爲本港最早的村落之一，居民多以耕田或捕魚爲生。

15 Hong Kong from the East, circa 1845
    by I.C. Bourne
    coloured lithograph, 34 × 56.2 cm

This view looking back on East Point and Hong Kong shows the original waterfront on the Causeway Bay area and Kellett Island. It may be compared with nos. 10 and 24.

15 從東區西眺維多利亞城之景，約一八四五年
    伯恩
    設色石版畫　34×56.2公分

圖中所見乃東角及港島中區之景，可見奇力島及銅鑼灣一帶在未填海前之景象。可與圖10及24比較。

16 Hong Kong Seen from the Anchorage, 1846
    by Lieutenant L.G. Heath
    coloured steel engraving, 12.5 × 203 cm

16 從港海眺望港島及九龍沿岸景色，一八四六年
    希思少校
    設色鋼版鐫刻版畫　12.5×203公分

This panorama was drawn on board the H.M.S. *Iris* and forms a 360° view of the harbour. This was published without colour in London by the Admiralty on 4th May 1847. It is a detailed picture and several early buildings and locations on Hong Kong are identified with captions.
See James Orange, *The Chater Collection*, p. 361.

此畫乃希思少校在停泊於港海內的「艾里斯」號輪上繪畫的。畫家環顧四周，並把所看見的景物詳盡地繪畫下來。英國海軍部曾於一八四七年五月四日刻印了不設色的版本。圖中還可看到一些本港早期的著名建築物，並附有說明。
可參閱 James Orange, *The Chater Collection*, 頁三六一。

17 View of Lyndhurst Terrace, Wellington Street, and Cochrane Street, Looking West from the Roman Catholic Church, 1846
by Murdoch Bruce, lithographed by A. Maclure
coloured lithograph, 22.5 × 35 cm

17 從羅馬天主堂西眺擺花街、威靈頓街及閣麟街景色，一八四六年
布魯士畫，麥克勞爾刻印
設色石版畫　22.5×35公分

This is one of a series of 12 views (nos. 17-28) lithographed in London by A. Maclure from original paintings by the architect, Murdoch Bruce, who was the Inspector of Buildings and Overseer of Roads for the Hong Kong administration. The buildings show that the area was still residential. Soldiers wearing bearskins and with fixed bayonets are marching on the foreground, and Wellington Street continues to Queen's Road and the sea front before later reclamation. The Old Union Church is shown in Hollywood Road at the upper left of the picture.

此套共十二幅石版畫（圖17至28），乃麥克勞爾在倫敦據布魯士的繪畫原作刻印的。布魯士曾爲本港的建築物及道路監督，此圖所見威靈頓街一帶主要是住宅區，全副武裝的軍隊正在進行操演；從威靈頓街向前望，可看見尚未塡海的海旁及港海的景色。圖中左方還可看到舊佑寧堂矗立於荷里活道之上。

18 Queen's Road Looking East from the Canton Bazaar, 1846
    by Murdoch Bruce, lithographed by A. Maclure
    coloured lithograph, 22.2 × 33.7 cm

18 從廣州市塲東眺皇后大道，一八四六年
    布魯士畫，麥克勞爾刻印
    設色石版畫　22.2×33.7公分

This view along what is now called Queensway shows interesting groups of Chinese and foreign pedestrians and an early horse-carriage. Oil street-lamps hang from some of the buildings.

此畫所見乃金鐘道景色，街上有華人，也有洋人，還可看到一輛馬車。道旁屋宇懸着點油的街燈。

19. Spring Gardens, 1846
by Murdoch Bruce, lithographed by A. Maclure
coloured lithograph, 22.8 × 34 cm

Spring Gardens, perhaps named after a district in London at the time, or from the stream which still flows down through it, is in the present Wan Chai. Spring Gardens Lane now runs between Johnston Road on the north and Queen's Road East in the south, and parallel to Lee Tung Street and Amoy Street. There is now extensive reclamation in front of the area illustrated. The Albany Godowns are shown in the background with Hospital Hill behind. The second house from the right was rented as Government House in Sir George Bonham's time.
See also K. Mattock, *This Is Hong Kong, Government House,* 1978, p. 21.

19　春園景色，一八四六年
　　布魯士畫，麥克勞爾刻印
　　設色石版畫　22.8×34公分

春園即今之灣仔，可能因該地區環境與倫敦春園相似，也可能因附近有一泉水而得名。春園街現位於皇后大道東、莊士敦道、利東街及廈門街之間。圖中所見地區沿岸現已填爲陸地。遠方爲雅賓利倉庫，其後方爲醫院山。圖中右方第二間建築物曾被租賃爲港督般含爵士的官邸。
可參閱 K. Mattock, *This is Hong Kong, Government House,* 一九七八年出版，頁二一。

20. Victoria Looking West from the Garden of the Chief Justice, 1846
    by Murdoch Bruce, lithographed by A. Maclure
    coloured lithograph, 24 × 37 cm

The residence of the first Chief Justice of Hong Kong was on the spur of Hospital Hill (the present Ruttonjee T.B. Sanatorium) Spring Gardens and the Albany Godowns are shown in the middle ground and the central district in the background.

20　從按察司官邸眺望維多利亞城，一八四六年
　　布魯士畫，麥克勞爾刻印
　　設色石版畫　24×37公分

本港首任按察司休姆爵士的官邸，乃位於醫院山山麓(今律敦治肺病療養院所在）。畫之中景爲春園，可看見雅賓利貨倉，遠方爲維多利亞城。

21. Aberdeen Street, Looking North, 1846
by Murdoch Bruce, lithographed by A. Maclure
coloured lithograph, 24.5 × 35.3 cm

This gives an interesting view down Aberdeen Street from just above
Wellington Street and Queen's Road. It shows European and Chinese
residents with the details of substantial buildings in the area.

21　鴨巴甸街北眺，一八四六年
布魯士畫，麥克勞爾刻印
設色石版畫　24.5×35.3公分

此圖所見乃自威靈頓街及皇后大道對上之鴨巴甸街向北眺之景色，圖
中尚可看到歐式住宅及華洋居民。

22. The Officers' Quarters Looking towards Victoria, 1846
by Murdoch Bruce, lithographed by A. Maclure
coloured lithograph, 26 × 35.5 cm

22　從美利兵房軍官宿舍西眺中區，一八四六年
布魯士畫，麥克勞爾刻印
設色石版畫　26×35.5公分

This fine view of part of Murray Barracks, soon after it was built in 1845, shows it in use as officers' quarters. The building still stands and is now used as a Government office. On the road which is still under construction, there are groups of officers, horses and a carriage and a water-buffalo in the foreground. Early buildings and Pedder's Hill are shown in the background and the line of the shore is fenced in with an oil street light on top.

美利樓原爲美利兵房的軍官宿舍，落成於一八四五年，該建築物迄今尚存，現爲政府某部門所在。圖中可見工人正忙於興築馬路，路上有一輛馬車，還有一頭水牛，遠處畢打山一帶建築物隱約可見，前方海旁圍上柵欄，並飾以點油的街燈。

23 The Residence of Lieutenant Governor the Honorable Major-General D'Aguilar, 1846
by Murdoch Bruce, lithographed by A. Maclure
coloured lithograph, 23.3 × 35 cm

23 德己立少將官邸，一八四六年
布魯士畫，麥克勞爾刻印
設色石版畫　23.3×35公分

This early view of the residence of the military commander is a detailed picture of Headquarter House, also later known as Flagstaff House, and completed just before Bruce made this painting. It has been the commander's residence until 1978 when the Victoria Barracks area was taken over by the Hong Kong Government. It is possibly the oldest residential building remaining in Hong Kong.

德己立少將官邸，又名旗杆屋，此圖當繪於該建築物落成後不久。在一九七八年維多利亞兵房移交港府前，該所建築物一直是駐港英軍司令的官邸，也可能是本港迄今尚存最有歷史價值的住宅。

24 Jardine, Matheson & Co., Looking Northwest from Causeway Bay, 1846
by Murdoch Bruce, lithographed by A. Maclure
coloured lithograph, 26 × 38 cm

This view shows the Jardine, Matheson buildings at East Point with foreign shipping at anchor. Jardines Matheson residences are shown on the left and Kellett Island and its fort on the right. The foreground shows Causeway Bay before the causeway or typhoon shelter (later Victoria Park) were built, but the cutting for the road is clear in the foreground with figures and a water-buffalo.

24 從銅鑼灣向西北眺望之渣甸洋行及倉庫，一八四六年
布魯士畫，麥克勞爾刻印
設色石版畫　26×38公分

圖中所見乃渣甸公司在東角的洋行及倉庫。碼頭前方停泊着數艘洋船，渣甸公司住宅在圖左，右方東角對開之小島乃奇力島，上有堡壘；畫的前方，即今銅鑼灣，後爲避風塘，現已填海成爲維多利亞公園。圖中還可見一條修好的馬路，上有行人及一頭水牛。

25 View of Wyndham Street, from the Post Office, 1846
by Murdoch Bruce, lithographed by A. Maclure
coloured lithograph, 24 × 35 cm

On the right is shown the first building for the Hong Kong Club which was founded in 1846 and was used until the Club moved to its present premises in 1898. The hill on the left was Pedder's hill, named after the first Harbour Master, with the flagstaff of the Harbour Master's Office just showing. Bruce shows here a horse-drawn carriage as in some of the views in this series. The Post Office from which the artist captured this view was about where China Building now is.

25 從郵政局南眺之雲咸街，一八四六年
布魯士畫，麥克勞爾刻印
設色石版畫　24×35公分

圖中右方建築物，乃舊香港會所，該會所成立於一八四六年，至一八九八年遷至現址。左方山岡為畢打山，乃因本港首任港務官而得名，港務官辦事處及旗杆，位於小岡頂，圖中的馬車，在布魯士的其他一些作品中亦可看到。郵政局即今華人行所在，此畫乃布魯士從該處南眺而繪畫的。

26 View of Queen's Road and the Harbour Looking West from Murray's Battery, 1846
by Murdoch Bruce, lithographed by A. Maclure
coloured lithograph, 24.3 × 34.8 cm

26 從美利炮台西眺港海及中區景色，一八四六年
布魯士畫，麥克勞爾刻印
設色石版畫　24.3×34.8公分

On the waterfront are shown godowns and the premises of Dent and Company with Dent's pier and an early seawall but little reclamation. On the other side of Queen's Road are the first Hong Kong Club building, Pedder's Hill and Harbour Master's Office.

海旁爲倉庫及顚地洋行的碼頭和辦公室，海旁已築有海堤，但並未填海。皇后道的另一邊是畢打山及港務官辦事處，岡下是舊香港會所。

27 Sai Wan, Hong Kong Looking East, 1846
by Murdoch Bruce, lithographed by A. Maclure
coloured lithograph, 22.5 × 38.8 cm

27 從西灣東眺港口，一八四六年
布魯士畫，麥克勞爾刻印
設色石版畫 22.5×38.8公分

The barracks shown here were built in the early 1840s but sickness among the troops caused them to be abandoned. The cows and goat shown here were to provide milk for the barracks. The whole area has now been reclaimed and developed.

此圖所見軍營興建於一八四〇年代早期，後因熱病猖獗，軍方撤離該地。圖中的牛羊，當為軍方飼養，整個地區現已填海，大廈如林。

28　South Side of Shek Pai Wan, Looking East, 1846
　　by Murdoch Bruce, lithographed by A. Maclure
　　coloured lithograph, 24 × 37.3 cm

This view shows part of the harbour of Aberdeen with Ap Lei Chau on the right with junks and houses. A Chinese temple and houses are in the middle distance with Brick Hill and the present Ocean Park area behind.

28　石排灣南岸東眺景色，一八四六年
　　布魯士畫，麥克勞爾刻印
　　設色石版畫　24×37.3公分

此圖所見乃香港仔漁港之一部份，右方爲鴨脷洲，島上有疏落的屋宇，港內有漁舟數艘，中景爲一小島，島上有廟宇及人家；遠方爲南朗山，其背後即今海洋公園所在。

29 Victoria from about Two Miles to the West, 1847
by George Robert West, lithographed by A. Maclure
coloured lithograph, 24 × 38.6 cm

An attractive view of the western entrance to the harbour from near Green
Island showing the harbour crowded with foreign shipping.
See also James Orange, *The Chater Collection*, page 362 and 389.

29 從中區以西二哩地方眺望維多利亞城，一八四七年
韋斯特畫，麥克勞爾刻印
設色石版畫 24×38.6公分

此畫當繪畫於青洲島附近，所見乃港島西面港口景色，港海內帆檣如
林。
可參閱 James Orange, *The Chater Collection*, 頁三六二及三八九。

30 View across Causeway Bay of Jardine, Matheson & Co. Premises at East Point and Kellett Island, 1840s
artist unknown
watercolour, 24 × 34.6 cm

30 東角渣甸洋行及奇力島，一八四○年代
畫家佚名
水彩畫　24×34.6公分

Similar view to nos. 10, 11 and 13, but not showing that any reclamation or road had been started.

此圖與圖10、11及13均描繪同一地點；圖中看不到有馬路或海堤的跡象。

31 Hong Kong from Kowloon, 1840s
lithographed by S. Fisher from drawing by Thomas Allom after original
sketch of Captain Stoddart, R.N.
coloured lithograph, 12.5 × 19 cm

The bay round from Tsim Sha Tsui in the right foreground has all been
included in the Chatham Road reclamation. A junk is shown under
construction and others are pulled up on the beach. Buildings on Hong
Kong Island are roughly drawn and foreign sailing ships are shown in the
harbour.
A plate from Allom and Wright's *China in a Series of Views*, see also
James Orange, *The Chater Collection*, pp. 353 and 379.

31 從九龍眺望港島之景，一八四〇年代
艾龍根據斯達特艦長的素描所繪畫，費希爾刻印
設色石版畫　12.5×19公分

圖中右方小岡爲尖沙咀，前方海灣，現已塡海，並修築爲漆咸道；工
人正忙於建造船隻，其中一些船隻被拖到岸上；背景爲香港島，島上
建築，繪畫得並不細緻。港海內停泊了不少洋船。
可參閱 Allom 及 Wright, *China in a Series of Views* 與及 James Orange,
The Chater Collection, 頁三五三及三七九。

32 Panorama of Hong Kong, 1851
   by Lieutenant Bellairs, R.N., lithographed by B. Walker
   coloured lithograph on canvas, 18 × 160 cm

An extensive view, somewhat similar to no. 16, from Lei Yu Mun on the
left to Green Island on the right. James Orange in *The Chater Collection*,
describes another copy of this lithograph and notes that it was 'Dedicated
by special permission to the Peninsular and Oriental Steam Navigation
Company'. Orange also refers to marginal identifications of the main
locations and buildings, and notes that it was 'Drawn on the spot by the
late Lt. Bellairs, R.N., Admiralty Agent', and lithographed by Day & Son
and published by Ackermann & Co. on 4th February 1851.
See James Orange, *The Chater Collection*, p. 364.

32 香港全景，一八五一年
   貝拉爾斯少校畫，沃爾克刻印
   設色帆布石版畫　18×160公分

此畫描寫鯉魚門至靑洲的全景，與圖16相似。 James Orange 在其著
作 *The Chater Collection* 收錄了另一幅完全一樣的版畫，並詳細描
述，還寫上「特准爲半島及東方船務公司所印製」字樣。 Orange 還
附註該版畫上主要建築物的名稱，並印上「貝拉爾斯少校繪於香港」
；該版畫乃由戴伊桑公司印製，並由阿克曼公司在一八五一年二月四
日出版。

可參閱 James Orange, *The Chater Collection* 頁三六四。

33 City of Victoria, Hong Kong Island, early 1850s
artist unknown
oil painting, 57 × 100 cm

33 維多利亞城遠眺，一八五〇年代早期
畫家佚名
油畫　57×100公分

A very detailed representation of the buildings from Spring Gardens on the east to Sai Ying Poon on the west. Government House, completed in 1855 is shown under construction and St John's Church, opened in 1849, is also visible.

畫中每一幢建築物的位置及形狀，皆非常精確，觀者能清楚地看到百多年前春園至西營盤的眞貌。圖中之草蓋屋爲建築中的督憲府，竣工於一八五五年。聖約翰教堂位於督憲府以東，該教堂於一八四九年落成。

34 Victoria and the Peak, 1855-60
artist unknown
watercolour, 44.1 × 77.1 cm

Easily identified are St John's Cathedral (1849); Government House (1855); Bishop's House (1851); the Roman Catholic Cathedral with twin spires; and Battery Path. Some reclamation seems to have taken place on the waterfront.

34 維多利亞城及山頂，一八五五至六○年
畫家佚名
水彩畫　44.1×77.1公分

畫中可清楚看到聖約翰教堂（一八四九年）；督憲府（一八五五年）；會督府（一八五一年）；羅馬天主教堂及其一對圓拱形之屋頂與及炮台徑。沿岸填海工程似正在進行。

35 Hong Kong from the East, 1855-60
by Marciano A. Baptista
watercolour, 36.4 × 52.6 cm

35 從東區眺望維多利亞城，一八五五至六○年
巴普蒂斯塔
水彩畫　36.4×52.6公分

Morrison Hill is shown in the foreground with Wan Chai (Little Bay) not reclaimed. The Central reclamation has been started but is unfinished in front of Dent's and Lindsay's premises as they opposed Sir John Bowring's praya scheme. A comparison picture to no. 38.

圖中前方爲摩利臣山，其後爲灣仔，其時尚未進行塡海，但中區塡海工程已經動工，由於顚地及林賽兩間洋行對保陵爵士的塡海計劃力加反對，故該兩間洋行前塡海工程尚未開始。可與圖38比較。

36 Hong Kong Island and City of Victoria, 1856 - 60
by Marciano A. Baptista
watercolour, 33 × 55 cm
signed

Some of the buildings are depicted with care and in detail. Well-known landmarks are the merchant houses of Lindsay & Co. Dent, Jardines and others along the waterfront with some unfinished reclamation in front of them. Among the buildings amid trees on the hills behind are Government House, the Bishop's House, Harbour Master's Office and Roman Catholic Cathedral.

36 港島及維多利亞城近景，一八五六至六〇年
巴普蒂斯塔
水彩畫　33×55公分
附有畫家署名

此畫前方建築物，繪畫得極其細緻，寫實性很高。林賽、顛地、渣甸等洋行皆為著名的陸標。此等商行前的塡海工程尚未完成。散佈在山腰的建築物包括督憲府、會督府、港務官辦事處及羅馬天主教堂。

37 Hong Kong Harbour with the Island in the Distance, 1858
    artist unknown
    gouache, 17 × 24 cm

37 港島及港海遠眺，一八五八年
    畫家佚名
    樹膠水彩畫　17×24公分

Finely executed in the style of Tingqua and with much detail. The view extends from East Point to the western entrance to the harbour and a variety of shipping is shown including a twin-funnelled paddle-steamer in the foreground.

此畫繪畫得十分細緻，畫風近關聯昌。畫中可見東角至港口西面入口處之景色，海港內帆檣如林，其中一艘為雙煙囪的美式輪船。

38 Hong Kong from Mid-levels Looking Northwest, circa 1858
    by Marciano A. Baptista
    watercolour, 39 × 60 cm

38 從半山俯瞰維多利亞城，約一八五八年
    巴普蒂斯塔
    水彩畫　39×60公分

An unusual view of central Victoria showing Murray Building and Victoria
Barracks; St Johns Cathedral; Government Offices, Government House;
and Stonecutter's Island and the Kowloon Hills in the background.

此畫之前景爲維多利亞城中部，建築物包括美利兵房、聖約翰敎堂、
輔政司署及督憲府。遠方爲昂船洲及逶迤的九龍羣山。

39 Hong Kong Harbour and Island from the Northwest, circa 1850s.
by C. Graham, engraved by A.H. Payne
aquatint, 11 × 16.7 cm

39 從西北方眺望港島及港海，約一八五〇年代
格雷厄姆繪畫，佩恩刻印
設色蝕刻版畫　11×16.7公分

Chinese junks and foreign shipping including a paddle-wheel steamer are shown against roughly-drawn buildings on the island.

港海內既有洋船——其中包括一艘美式輪船，也有中國式帆船，港島上的屋宇，並不寫實。

40 Victoria from the North, late 1850s
artist unknown
oil painting, 53.2 × 147.5 cm

40 從北方眺望維多利亞城，一八五〇年代晚期
畫家佚名
油畫　53.2×147.5公分

This view extends from Lei Yu Mun to the western end of Hong Kong Island. Some of the well-known landmarks which appear are Jardines premises and flagstaff at East Point (started in 1841); Morrison Institute (1843); St Johns Cathedral (opened 1849); Government Offices (1848); and Government House (1855)

畫中可見從鯉魚門至港島西區的景色，可辨認的陸標包括位於東角的渣甸洋行及旗杆（興建於一八四一年）；馬禮遜教育會（一八四三年）；聖約翰教堂（落成於一八四九年）；輔政司署（一八四八年）及督憲府（一八五五年）。

41 Hong Kong Harbour and Island, circa 1861
artist unknown
watercolour, 18 × 22 cm

41 港島及港海，約一八六一年
畫家佚名
水彩畫　18×22公分

There is much detail in the buildings and a variety of shipping. St John's Cathedral is clearly seen in the centre of the picture and the signal station erected in 1861 is visible on the top of Victoria Peak.

此畫繪畫得頗爲細緻，所有建築物，均很寫實。港海內船隻種類很多，圖之中央爲聖約翰敎堂，山頂的訊號台，建於一八六一年。

42 Elevation of the Hong Kong Mint, 1864
    by Arthur Kinder
    coloured engraving, 59 × 112 cm

42 香港造幣廠，一八六四年
    金特
    設色金屬刻版畫　59×112公分

The Mint was located at East Point and opened in 1866 and the first Hong Kong silver dollars were issued in June. However, it was financially unsuccessful and closed in February 1868. All the machinery was sold to Japan and may have had some influence on the size and design of the Japanese yen at the time. Jardine, Matheson & Co. later used the site for a sugar refinery after which Sugar Street in Causeway Bay is named.

香港造幣廠位於銅鑼灣，在一八六六年開幕；同年六月，第一批銀圓面世。該廠因業務不佳，於一八六八年二月結束，機器售予日本。日本當時所生產的銀幣，當有不少用此等機器製造。廠址則賣給怡和，後來乃於該地興建怡和糖廠，此乃銅鑼灣糖街得名的來源。

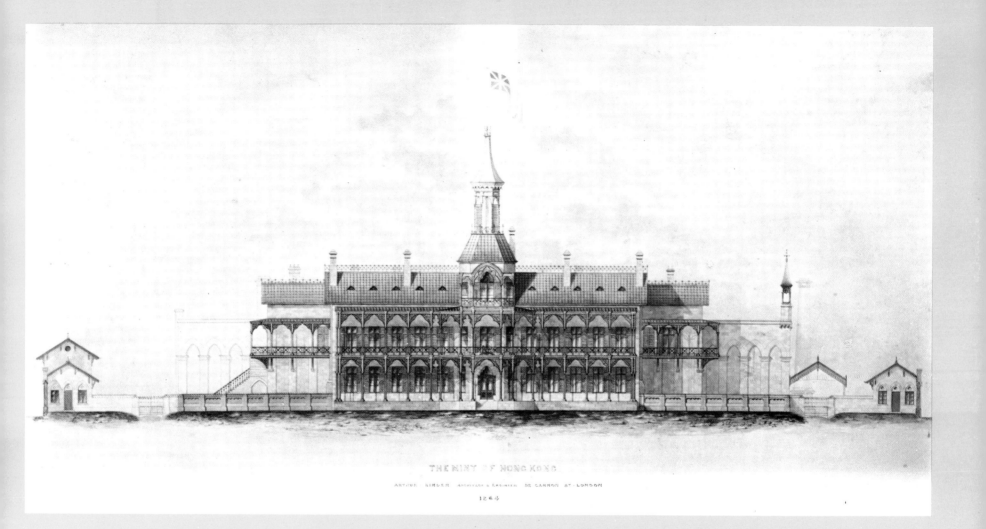

THE MINT OF HONG KONG

ARTHUR KIMBER ARCHITECT & ENGINEER 56 CANNON ST LONDON

1864

43 Victoria from the Harbour, 1860s
   by H.C. Gandill
   watercolour, 41.5 × 69 cm
   signed

Steam and sailing ships are shown in the harbour and, on the island, the buildings and road construction have reached to the Mid-levels and trees and vegetation cover parts of the hills. The tip of Tsim Sha Tsui is just visible in the foreground.

43 從港海眺望維多利亞城，一八六〇年代
   甘迪
   水彩畫　41.5×69公分
   附有畫家署名

港海內帆檣林立，有中國式帆船，也有外國輪船。此畫清楚顯示半山區屋宇已有顯著增加。太平山部份已爲樹木所掩蓋，前方可看到尖沙咀的尖端。

44 Hong Kong and the Harbour, 1860s
artist unknown
oil painting, 43.2 × 57.2 cm

44 香港島及港海，一八六〇年代
畫家佚名
油畫　43.2×57.2公分

Most of the large ships are steamships. The details of the buildings are not very accurate but the major landmarks are easily recognizable and the signal station on the Peak is also just visible.

港海內的輪船已有所增加；畫中建築物繪畫得並不精確，但一些主要的陸標尚不難辨認。山頂上的訊號台也清晰可見。

45 A Side Street, Hong Kong, 1860s
by E. Hildebrandt
reproduction of a watercolur, 34 × 24 cm
signed

45 港島某街道，一八六〇年代
希爾德布蘭特
水彩畫複本　34×24公分
附有畫家署名

This colourful picture depicts a summer afternoon scene of a typical side street probably running north-south from Queen's Road. The characters on the signboards are not exact, but the clothes drying on bamboo poles are characteristic.

此圖所見乃皇后大道中的橫街，時值酷暑，烈日當空，招牌上的字，祇是胡亂塗寫，街道兩旁掛滿曬晾在竹竿上的衣服，是本港街道常見的景象。

46 Queen's Road, Hong Kong, circa 1860s
by E. Hildebrandt
reproduction of a watercolour, 27.5 × 38.2
signed

46 皇后大道，約一八六〇年代
希爾德布蘭特

水彩畫複本　27.5×38.2公分
附有畫家署名

Probably Queen Road West showing typical two and three storey shops built out on pillars over the pavements. The pedestrians are using umbrellas as shields from the summer sun indicated by the strong light and shade.

相信是皇后大道西，圖中樓宇皆爲兩三層的店舖，屋柱伸出行人道。行人皆持傘而行，以遮擋烈日。

Hongkong   E. Wildbrandt

47　View of Hong Kong from the East, 1875
artist unknown
woodblock engraving, 15.2 × 22.9 cm

47　從東區遠眺港島，一八七五年
畫家佚名
木刻版畫　15.2×22.9公分

A nicely composed picture showing extensive building in the central and western parts of the city and some reclamation. Sailing and steam ships are seen in the harbour. The Europeans at the tea table are probably in Jardines' Garden above East Point.

此畫構圖甚佳，中區及西區已屋宇林立，部份地區經已填海。港海內有帆船，也有輪船，前景可見數歐人在喝茶，該地可能乃位於東角小岡上的渣甸私邸花園。

48 Hong Kong Island and Harbour, 1870s
artist unknown
watercolour, 16.8 × 24 cm

48 香港港海景色，一八七〇年代
畫家佚名
水彩畫　16.8×24公分

The ships and buildings are depicted in detail. The development of steamships and the opening of the Suez Canal in 1869 brought better and increased commerce and communication to Hong Kong and many shipping lines established their services at about this time. The Pedder Street Clock Tower (1862) and the Peak Signal Station are clearly seen, but there is no sign of the Peak Tram (1888).

畫家精確地描繪了各種船隻及建築物。輪船業的發展與及一八六九年蘇彝士運河通航後，本港貿易更形蓬勃，航運公司紛紛開業。圖中可清楚看見畢打街大鐘樓（一八六二年）及山頂訊號台，但仍未見纜車軌道（一八八八年）。

49 Victoria from the North, late 19th century
artist unknown
oil painting, 41.5 × 73.5 cm

49 從北面眺望維多利亞城，十九世紀晚期
畫家佚名
油畫 41.5×73.5公分

Although the buildings are not very accurate the major landmarks are easily recognizable, including Flagstaff House, St John's Cathedral, Government House and the Pedder Street Clock Tower. Much of the praya, Des Voeux Road, reclamation has been completed.

畫中景物，雖非寫實，但一些較重要的建築，尚不難辨認，其中包括旗杆屋、聖約翰教堂、督憲府及位於畢打街的大鐘樓。德輔道海旁的填海工程已接近完成階段。

50 View of Hong Kong, late 19th century
    artist unknown
    oil painting, 40.5 × 56.5 cm

50 港島一景，十九世紀晚期
    畫家佚名
    油畫　40.5×56.5公分

This rather imprecise picture shows sailing ships in the harbour. The island in the middle ground is probably Kellett Island and the chimney to the left on Hong Kong Island may be connected with the sugar refinery.

此油畫繪畫得並不精確，前景是港海中各種船隻。圖中心的小島爲奇力島，而位於港島左方的烟卤或是當時渣甸糖廠所在。

51 Wellington Street and Lyndhurst Terrace, Hong Kong, late 19th century
by C. Andrasi, lithographed by J. Laurens
coloured lithograph, 30 × 44 cm

51 香港威靈頓街及擺花街，十九世紀晚期
安德烈西畫，勞倫刻印
設色石版畫　30×44公分

This rather fanciful view is an interesting comparison with Murdoch Bruce's more formal and exact style (no. 17). The lively Chinese street scenes include an operatic stage on the right, shops, tradesmen, and a horse and cart in the distance.

此圖富於想像，與布魯士偏重寫實的繪畫比較（圖17），倍覺趣味盎然。街景富有生活氣息。圖右方為一戲台，遠處則為各式店舖、商販及馬匹。

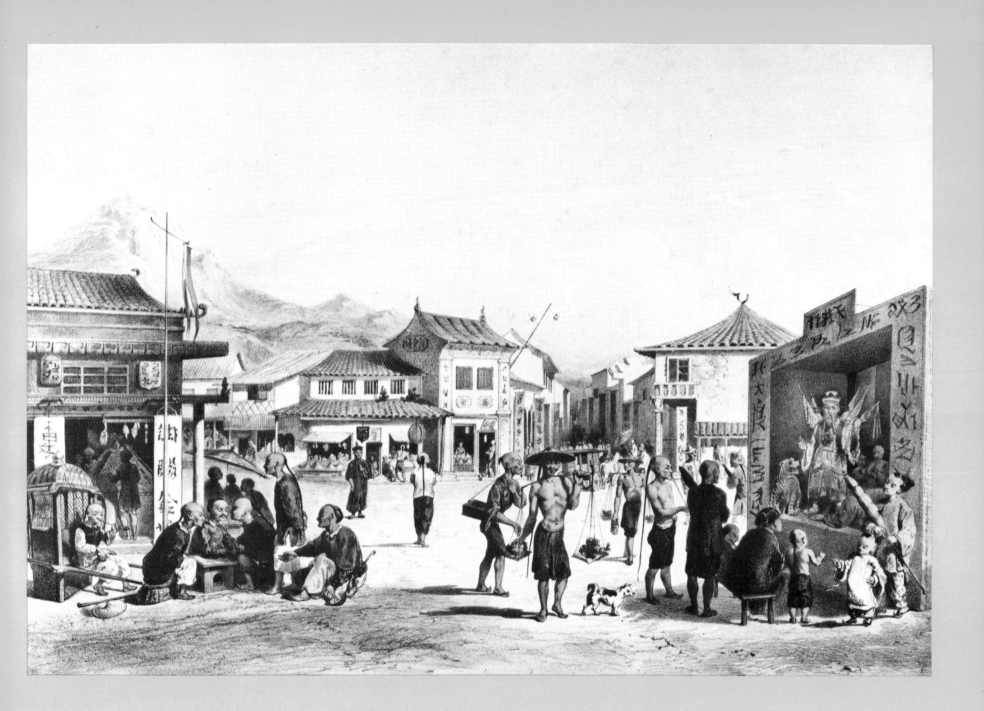

52 Hong Kong Harbour from above Shau Kei Wan, late 19th century
artist unknown
watercolour, 13 × 48.9 cm

52 筲箕灣下眺景色，十九世紀晚期
畫家佚名
水彩畫　13×48.9公分

A steamer is shown in the harbour but the other boats are mainly junks. Shau Kei Wan is still noted for its shipbuilding and repairing and is a fishing village. The construction of a road in 1864 and the tramway in 1904 helped to make the area more accessible.

港海中有一輪船，其餘皆爲漁船。時至今日，筲箕灣仍爲一著名漁港，並以造船及修船業著稱。自一八六四年馬路修成，及一九〇四年電車開始服務，該地交通乃較前方便。

53 Hong Kong Harbour and Island, late 19th century
artist unknown
oil painting, 22.8 × 30.5 cm

53 港島全景，十九世紀晚期
畫家佚名
油畫 22.8×30.5公分

This picture is interesting for the early residences shown on the Peak which became more popular as a summer resort in the last quarter of the nineteenth century. The route of the Peak Tram (1888) is also visible as well as the Bowen waterworks carrying water from Tai Tam Reservoir along the line of Bowen road. The first City Hall next to the old Hong Kong and Shanghai Bank building start the line of waterfront buildings on the left, and the Hong Kong hotel and Jardines offices are shown at the end of Pedder Street with the Clock Tower behind. The ships in the harbour are mainly steamships.

這幅畫最使人感到興趣的是描繪了早期山頂區的建築。十九世紀晚期，該地區漸成為避暑勝地。圖中亦可見纜車軌（一八八八年）及自大潭水塘沿寶雲道建築的寶雲道引水道。舊大會堂位於舊上海滙豐銀行旁邊，此為中區海旁左方的第一幢建築物。畢打街盡頭乃香港酒店及渣甸洋行，其後為大鐘樓。港海中所見船隻幾盡為輪船。

54 The Botanical Gardens, Hong Kong, late 19th century
artist unknown
coloured engraving, 18 × 22.5 cm

54 香港植物公園，十九世紀晚期
畫家佚名
設色金屬刻版畫　18×22.5公分

The gardens were begun in the time of Sir John Bowring and extended by Sir John Pope Hennessy. The statue shown here is probably that of Sir Arthur Kennedy (governor 1872-1877) which was erected in 1887 but was removed in World War II. Residences at mid-levels and on the Peak are shown in the background. Three lampposts are shown to light the paths on the garden.

植物公園始建於港督保陵爵士在任期間，其後軒尼詩爵士又撥地增建。畫中所見乃港督堅尼地爵士（任期由一八七二至一八七七年）的銅像，設置於一八八七年，第二次世界大戰時被移去。此畫的背景爲建於半山及山頂的樓宇，畫中的三條燈柱乃爲照明園中小徑而設。

55 Hong Kong Harbour and Island, end of 19th century
artist unknown
oil painting, 27.8 × 55.7 cm

55 海港與港島，十九世紀末期
畫家佚名
油畫　27.8×55.7公分

Further residential development is shown on the Peak and the route of the Peak Trams (1888) is just seen. There is extensive building at mid-levels and on the waterfront the praya reclamation in front of the first City Hall is under construction.

圖中可見圍繞山頂的建築發展，山頂纜車（一八八八年）亦剛啓行。半山及沿岸的樓宇更形稠密。舊大會堂的前方正展開塡海工程。

56 Queen's Road East, end of 19th century
artist unknown
coloured engraving, 17.8 × 14.2 cm

56 皇后大道東，十九世紀末期
畫家佚名
設色金屬刻版畫　17.8×14.2公分

The temple on the right opposite the Sikh policeman is probably the Tai Wong Temple which still survives in good condition. The Chinese characters are fanciful but are typical shop signs hung on the pillars.

圖中右方所見乃灣仔的大王廟，此廟迄今尚存，廟宇的對面，還可看見一個印籍警察。在廟旁石柱上的文字雖非寫實，但皆爲典型招牌設計。

57 House on the Way to Repulse Bay, 1926
    by Alfred Lane
    watercolour, 54 × 75 cm
    signed

57 淺水灣附近之別墅，一九二六年
    萊恩
    水彩畫　54×75公分
    附有畫家署名

This country house or lodge built on its granite foundation with numerous street lights and sweeping entrance has long since disappeared but appears to have been newly constructed when this picture was made. Repulse Bay was still a remote area only reached by sea until the road was extended there in 1917.

畫中所見的是建築在花崗巖石地基上的別墅，及附近所點綴的街燈及寬敞的大門入口，那時大概剛裝修完竣，但此別墅現已不復存在。在一九一七年以前，公路還未修建至淺水灣，只有水路可達。

58 Conduit Road Residence, 1926
by Alfred Lane
watercolour, 54 × 74 cm
signed

Many elegant mansions were built at mid-levels to escape from the increasing congestion and heat of the central district, which became used more for commercial and office premises than for residence. The mid-levels had the advantage over the Peak of easier access by road and was less affected by low cloud and humidity. The palatial building shown in the picture was originally built as the residence of a wealthy Chinese merchant. It later became the Foreign Correspondents Club. The building has been replaced by high-rise apartments.

58　干讀道豪華住宅，一九二六年
萊恩
水彩畫　54×74公分
附有畫家署名

在中區逐漸發展成為商業區後，人們為遠離繁囂的市中心和減少夏天的悶熱，紛紛於半山興建豪華住宅。半山區的居住環境比山頂更勝一籌，這裡交通方便，視野清晰，空氣乾爽。此圖所見之豪華樓宇，乃當時某華籍殷商之住宅，後改為外國通訊社辦事處，現已改建為高樓。

Alfred
1926 Lang

Printed by Allied Printers Limited
1-5 Tonnochy Road
Hong Kong